THE NEXT BIG THING

HOW TO FIND YOUR NEXT BUSINESS IDEA AND FAST TRACK YOUR SUCCESS

By Entrepreneur Encyclopedia

Visit

www.Entrepedia.co/FreeBooks
to receive Entrepedia books for FREE

www.Entrepedia.co/QuickStart
for your Entrepreneur Quick Start Guide

ABOUT ENTREPRENEUR ENCYCLOPEDIA

Our aim is to provide you with the knowledge you'll need to start a business from $0 and grow it to $100k per month in passive income.

You'll learn how to pick your niche, build a brand, drive free and paid traffic, deliver massive value, market your work, hire and outsource, systematize your process, scale and more.

Your destiny is up to you. Money can help you grow quickly but you don't need it. No banker or VC can tell you your idea is not good enough.

What you'll need to do is test the theories you develop, fail quickly and find products customers will pay you to create before spending a dime. Each step of the way you will be building an audience that will snowball into your inevitable success.

Being an entrepreneur requires you to learn an enormous amount of information on an endless variety of topics. You must find what's working, put your own spin on it, create massive value and give it to as many people as possible.

Today it's easier than ever to start a lifestyle business or grow a billion dollar company. But like anything, it requires effort, determination and a strong desire to help the world move in a positive direction.

Entrepreneur Encyclopedia is the shortest route to your dreams. Our books are designed to help you understand everything you need to know about each topic in under an hour.

Each one of our books will help you move your business forward in a vital area. Think of us like a mentor helping you break through plateaus and discover leading edge paths by showing you how to properly leverage today's best technology to be successful.

GIVING BACK

Entrepreneur Encyclopedia has taken the copyright off everything we publish and donate our material directly to the public domain. Powerful information like this should be available to anyone so they can benefit without restriction. Wisdom is for sharing. You can read the details on our uncopyright disclaimer.

EE is also teaming up with Kiva.org to help fund new projects by entrepreneurs in developing countries. Our aim is to provide 5% of our net sales to funding micro loans for people with a vision but without the ability to get loans from VCs or the banking system.

To minimize our footprint and help restore forests around the globe we are planting a tree for every 10 hardcover books we sell. You can read more about our mission at the back of this book. We pledge to put our clients and our world ahead of our profits.

Thanks for choosing Entrepreneur Encyclopedia and helping us help the planet.

Sincerely,

Travis & The Entrepedia Team

Uncopyright 2017 by Smart Reads, Inc. No rights reserved worldwide. Any part of this publication may be reproduced or transmitted in any form without the prior written consent of the publisher.

Disclaimer: The publisher and author make no representations or warranties with respect to the accuracy or completeness of these contents and disclaim all warranties for a particular purpose. The author or publisher is not responsible for how you use this information.

TABLE OF CONTENTS

Foreword	2
Introduction	4
PART I: DESIGNING YOUR MISSION	7
Chapter 1: Prepping For The Journey	8
Chapter 2: The Future Test	10
Chapter 3: Back in Time	15
Chapter 4: Your Unfair Advantage	20
Chapter 5: Sticking To Your Mission	26
PART II: DEVELOPING YOUR IDEA	28
Chapter 6: Don't Put The Cart Before The Horse	29
Chapter 7: Germinating Your Idea	33
Chapter 8: The Single Sentence	40
Chapter 9: Sharing and Observing Your Idea	43
PART III: CHECKING OUT YOUR BUSINESS ENVIRONMENT	50
Chapter 10: Identifying Your Core Audience	51
Chapter 11: Mapping Your Market	54
Chapter 12: Understanding Your Customer	62
Chapter 13: Solving Problems	73
PART IV: WILL YOUR DREAM FLY?	76
Chapter 14: Validating Your Solution	77
Chapter 15: How To Validate Your Idea	80

Chapter 16: Examples of Validation   90
Chapter 17: Prepping For Your Launch   96

Conclusion   100
Mission   103

FOREWORD

Did you know that the Foreword is one of the least read parts of any book? Yet here you are, probably asking yourself why you are even bothering with this page.

It could be that you are one of those methodical readers, or maybe you are still wondering whether this book is worth your time. You still question whether this book can help you launch that grand business idea you've been incubating.

Rather than spend your time watching TV shows and sports, you can spare a couple of hours every week consuming content that will add value to your financial future.

Unlike other entrepreneurial books, The Next Big Thing contains summarized lessons that will help you jumpstart your business. Consider this a concise and frank checklist you need before getting your business idea off the ground.

One of the first things to do is examine whether the idea you have in mind is a good fit for you. Most entrepreneurs tend to put more emphasis on the viability of the idea itself without verifying whether it's something they love to do. To make your business a success, you have to put yourself into the equation, and this book shows you how to stop guessing and actually start your journey based on facts.

Prepare for a practical, down-to-earth, and simple way of making your idea the next big thing!

INTRODUCTION

If you have ever folded paper airplanes before, you know there is a right way to do it and a wrong way to do it. For a kid who is doing it for the first time, they will be tempted to rush through the paper folding process because they are excited and just want to see the plane fly. More often than not, the end result looks nothing like a plane - with wings out of place and so forth. This is how many entrepreneurs approach their business ideas.

You are reading this book because you are considering launching your own project and want to watch it fly. This book is meant to help you fold the paper the right way.

As a budding entrepreneur, you have your personal dreams and ambitions. There is a "why" that drives you to push forward and make things work. You may have a picture in your head of what you want to achieve but the path to getting there is still hazy.

Maybe you have read hundreds of business books and you are now more confused than ever about where to begin. You could be apprehensive about spending precious time and money on a project that won't succeed. It is important that you don't make assumptions and rush the process like a child would with their first paper plane. This is what this book will teach you: how to do things the right way and visualize where you are going.

You need to realize that ideas are nothing but myths. You can decide to make assumptions about your business idea, but at the end of the day, your results will determine whether you were right or wrong. Why wait until after the launch to determine the outcome when you can test the assumptions beforehand? This is why experimentation is critical to discovering the truth. Imagine if you could create a miniature version of your idea, place it in a controlled environment, and test all your theories. This would enable you to better understand the process and gain confidence when making real-life decisions.

Maybe you have one specific idea or several running through your brain. Having great ideas is cool, but without action, they are just wasting space in your head. Most people don't actualize their ideas because they lack direction, can't settle on one idea and make it work, feel unqualified, lack the resources, or are afraid of failure. Whatever the reason is, this book will show you the steps necessary to start taking action.

From here on out, you will take an in-depth look at the quality of your ideas. You will run your ideas through various experiments and tests to see whether they hold up or fall flat. Consider this book as a series of tests where your ideas are tested, not you. Even if your idea fails, it's still a win for you because then you will have a clearer picture of what **not** to do. If your idea passes the tests, you will have much greater confidence moving forward.

In all honesty, the two biggest flaws to any business are:

- Putting money ahead of serving customers
- Rushing into things with no clear blueprint

This book will teach you how to avoid these two entrepreneurial mistakes.

This book is divided into five parts, with each part covering a critical aspect of starting a project, from validating the idea to launching the business. You will learn how to build your business the smart way so you can use your gifts and talents to benefit the world.

We are grateful that you have allowed us to work together with you to make your dream business a reality!

PART I: DESIGNING YOUR MISSION

In this section, you'll need to conduct a few experiments to ensure your business idea aligns with your life goals. It is important that you succeed both in life as well as in business if you want genuine happiness. This section will be a form of self-examination to help you avoid becoming a wealthy yet unfulfilled entrepreneur.

CHAPTER 1: PREPPING FOR THE JOURNEY

Every entrepreneur desires a life of freedom, where you live according to your own terms. The truth is that while everybody wishes they could live this way, the entrepreneur has gone beyond wishing and has taken action to make it a reality.

However, there is an increasingly common phenomenon known as "the unhappy yet wealthy entrepreneur." There are many people out there who have started great businesses, make millions of dollars every year, and yet are totally miserable. The question you need to ask yourself is how does a person get to this point?

Now, there is nothing wrong with being unsatisfied with the way your business is going from time to time. Running a business involves ups and downs that you have to deal with on a regular basis. There will be failures and setbacks. However, an entrepreneur who is unhappy with their life signifies there is a huge problem somewhere.

One of the problems that many people fail to recognize is that having a successful business doesn't automatically translate to a successful life. There are people right now who are leaving their jobs or careers to start businesses, thinking this is the cool way to live. Yet these people have no idea what this cool life looks like! Just because you had a great idea doesn't mean you are the right person to build that business. You have to be certain that the idea is aligned with your personal goals.

This is why you need to design your mission first. You should be able to define all your life goals and whether your business idea will support these goals. If they don't align, then prepare for a rich but unhappy life. Why would you want to spend your money and time building something that makes money but drains you of your happiness and life?

To some, this may be selfish thinking, considering that a business should solve someone else's problem, not your own life goals. But what you need to think about is the level of passion you will be able to sustain in the long run. Without understanding why you are in that particular business, your energy will dissipate, especially when things get rough.

Designing your mission involves undertaking a number of tests and exercises to help define your future. These tests will also show you how your target idea either supports or contradicts your life goals. If you discover that your idea is fully aligned with your goals, you should proceed to the next part of the book. If they don't match, consider that a win because at least you found out early enough. Find another idea and go through the tests again. These tests are quick and simple. Make sure you have pen and paper handy.

CHAPTER 2: THE FUTURE TEST

This is your first test, but as mentioned before, there is no need to worry. It's a win-win, regardless of the outcome.

Why is it called the future test? This test requires you to sit down and travel five years into the future. Let's assume that your future self is extremely happy and fulfilled, both financially and personally. You need to see every different aspect of your life, and then ask yourself what made your life so amazing in the first place.

This test is designed to help you see whether your ideal future is aligned with your business goals. Most entrepreneurs tend to begin a new project, get bored, and then move on to another idea. By going through this test, you minimize the chances of this happening to you.

But why are 5 years and not 10 or maybe two? Five years is a good number because it is not too short or too long. Anything more than five years may end up being impractical because anything can happen in the far-off future. If you consider anything less than five years, you would probably start thinking small rather than create a big vision to strive for.

It is important that you go through this exercise right now rather than postpone it. You will determine a 5-year plan and how the business idea you have fits into that plan. If they don't fit, keep the plan intact but change the idea.

Sure, writing the plan down is the common way to do it, but visualizing the plan infuses emotions that bring out honesty and pragmatism.

Exercise
The aim of this exercise is to identify who you are and how your idea fits you. If you start implementing your idea without knowing who you are, what you want, or your core values, you will end up either never launching the business or crashing and burning. Either way, you will not get to your destination.

Step 1: Prepare your worksheet
Grab a plain piece of paper and fold it to create four equal quadrants.

Step 2: Write down the four key areas of your life
Each quadrant represents an important part of your life. For example, you can have family, business, health, and finances. Just note down at the top of the quadrant what you believe is most important to you.

Step 3: Identify the reasons why life would be great five years into your future
This is the part you should enjoy the most. Take each of the four categories you have listed and write down examples of things that would make that area of your life awesome. Don't be afraid of thinking big. Just write what an amazing future would look like in those four areas.

Write as many details as you can. You don't have to order them a certain way. Write down whatever comes to mind. You can choose to be general or zoom into details. Once you finish with one quadrant, move to the next one and write down everything you can think of. If you run out of paper, then grab another sheet.

Let's use the example of the four categories we mentioned earlier; Family, Business, Health, and Finances.

For the family, you could write:
- I am happily married and love my wife and kids.
- My children are all healthy, growing fast, and learning entrepreneurial skills.
- We travel to different parts of the country on vacation.
- We communicate well with each other even when angry.

For business, you could write:
- I am a bestselling author of five entrepreneurial books.
- I run a charity organization for inner city kids, where they are taught business skills.
- I receive hundreds of fan mail from entrepreneurs thanking me for inspiring them to success.
- I take days off to vacation with my family whenever I want.

For health, you could write:
- I live a stress-free life.
- I am happy and full of energy.
- I eat healthily and so does my family.
- I have run a full marathon and training for another triathlon.

For finances, you could write:
- We live in a mortgage-free home.
- The kids have college funds prepared.
- Our expenses are in control.
- We donate hundreds of thousands of dollars to charities every year.
- Our emergency fund can cover expenses for two years.

The above are just examples. Whatever you choose to write down, make sure that you are being authentic to your inner self. The next step is to read through what you have written. Remember that this sheet of paper will define the kind of decisions you make because it details the kind of person you want to become.

This process of projecting your future life now can be emotional for some people. Once you realize that you are so far from where you need to be, it can get hard to deal with, but at least you learned this early on. You can still change some things around and achieve what you truly want out of your life.

There's one more thing. Keep this sheet of paper close because you are going to need it later on.

Your Business Idea
Now that you have an idea of what your life will look like in the future, what about your business idea? Does it fit into your future narrative? It may not be possible to know the outcome of your potential business idea, but you can still imagine what the business will be like in the future.

It is now time to see whether your idea doesn't fit into your future life. For those whose idea is aligned with their future self, you have more tests awaiting you, just to refine the idea you already have. It is a very satisfying experience knowing that every business decision you make fits into your future. Making certain decisions, especially big moneymaking opportunities, becomes easier. If you value spending time with your family, you won't be tempted by a million-dollar venture that takes you away from your loved ones.

For those who discover that their potential idea doesn't fit in their future, there are tough choices that must be made. You can decide to keep the idea you currently have and keep reading the book or you can choose to dump the idea, pick a new one, and run it through the test. The good thing is that you still have the sheet of paper containing what your future life will look like. It is still a win-win for you.

Let's move on to the second test!

CHAPTER 3: BACK IN TIME

The first test involved going five years into the future. In the second test, you will be going back in time, except this time the number of years will depend on when you were first employed.

Consider this a history test but without the essays, wars, or famous speeches. You will be taking a look at the past in order to forge a greater future. You will be required to remember all your past jobs, work positions, and volunteering that you did. It's like creating a resume but trying to dig deeper so you can identify some of the patterns that define the real you and your professional preferences.

This chronological roadmap will help you see where your weaknesses and strengths lie, and what things you are attracted to. All this information will help you determine how the business idea you have aligns with your personality and your past trajectory. As always, we shall walk you through the test and then look at some questions that will clarify whatever you will have written down.

One thing that you need to know is that it is okay if your idea seems misaligned with the choices you made in the past. You don't have to get rid of it because maybe you are supposed to change something. If all your past jobs were in engineering, that doesn't mean you have to continue in the same industry. The goal of the following exercise is to take the positive experiences of past jobs and infuse them into the potential idea you have. Maybe some of the skills you learned in engineering could be used to support your idea, and even help modify it further.

Remember that the tests in this book do not have wrong answers. It is all about self-learning and watching out for any warning signs. The lessons learned in this first part of the book will serve you well, especially if you get a new idea and have to redo the tests.

Exercise
Just as before, grab a plain piece of paper and follow the instructions below.

Step 1:
Write down your first job. If you are still searching for one or you are a student, write down an internship or anything that required you to show up consistently.

Step 2: When was it?
Underneath your first job, note down when you were hired there, for example, from 2002 – 2005.

Step 3: What did you love about it?
What did you love about your first job? Write down three answers. Did you like your coworkers? Was it fun? Was the schedule flexible? Maybe you enjoyed being a team leader or networking with influential people.

Step 4: What was your best memory?
The answer can be brief or as long as you want. You can go ahead and explain something that painted you in a good light in front of your work colleagues. Maybe you did something that your boss noticed and praised you for.

Step 5: What did you not like?
What are some of the things about that first job that you hated? Write down three things, for example, wearing ugly uniforms, being disrespected, or cleaning the floors.

Step 6: Rating
Now it is time to rate the job experience on a scale of A to E.

A – It was awesome!
B – Somewhat enjoyable
C – OK
D – Not enjoyable
E - Terrible

The majority of people who engage in this particular exercise learn so much about themselves. It gives you an opportunity to discover why you like certain things and not others, and this enables you to piece together who you are.

Now that you have completed all six steps for one past life experience, do the same for another two experiences. They can be jobs, projects, or places you have volunteered. Just follow the same steps as the first one. By the way, if you feel up to it, go ahead and add more experiences just to get a clearer picture of who you are.

By simply reading through the timeline of your past experiences, you can begin to see your likes and motivations. If what you enjoyed doing back then aligns with what you like doing today, you are on the right track. If you enjoyed being in a leadership role and influencing people and events, you are definitely cut out for entrepreneurship.

Take another look at what you have written down. Do you see any patterns? Look at the score rating for the first experience and compare it with the rest of the scores for the other experiences. Is the score improving or getting worse as time goes by?

Based on the patterns you see from your past, here are three more questions that you can ask yourself. In this case, you don't have to write your answers down. However, it's best to think deeply about your answers.

1. Name two things that serve as primary motivators for the work you engaged in the past.
2. Are those motivators still a factor in the work you do today?
3. In what way can you shape your future business into a venture that you enjoy while staying motivated?

The third question above is the main reason for performing the exercise. You need to identify how your potential business idea aligns with what you like to do professionally. In other words, you should be able to visualize what will be required of you and compare that with where you want to go in life. Ultimately, you will have a greater chance of achieving success.

It is important to understand that establishing a business is never a straightforward process. There will always be good times and bad times, and often these peaks and troughs follow each other immediately. Surviving the highs and lows requires a high degree of endurance that can only come from having genuine motivation to carry you through.

What you need to constantly watch out for are misalignments between who you are and the kind of business you are planning to engage in. When you focus on a business that will make you a lot of money but isn't part of your motivations, you will find it easier to quit when the going gets tough. This is not the way to go for an entrepreneur who wants to be successful. Always make sure your motivations and your business are a good fit.

CHAPTER 4: YOUR UNFAIR ADVANTAGE

In this chapter, you'll learn the final and most important exercise of Designing Your Mission. We have now come back to the present after time traveling a little bit. For some of you, your business idea remains an idea, but it has undergone some kind of metamorphosis after being taken through tests in the previous chapters. As we proceed deeper into the book, your idea will want to transform into something else, so don't resist it. If the idea looks like a non-starter and needs to be dropped, just accept that reality too.

You are going to engage in a small thought exercise here. We want you to see yourself walking down a long hallway and into a room. In the middle of the room are five seated individuals, whom you soon discover are renowned venture capitalists. You are required to stand before them and answer a few questions about your business idea.

At the moment, you won't be asked to pitch your idea. We will work on that in the next part of the book. For now, you will deal with something a bit different. The majority of entrepreneurs focus on the product or service they are offering and its benefits to consumers, and rightly so. However, entrepreneurship goes way beyond that.

How many times have you seen an entrepreneur with a wonderful product but they fail to make it work for them? This is a common occurrence. Conversely, how many times have you seen a mediocre product become accepted and perform well in the market? This happens all the time, too. You see, it is not just about the product you are pitching to the market. It is also about you, the individual behind the product. Though it may have seemed that the tests we have gone through in the previous exercises were focusing on your idea, in fact they were designed to reveal more about you.

As you stand there in front of the five venture capitalists, one of them looks straight at you and says, "Whatever it is you are selling, I can probably pay someone else to do right now. Why do I need to work with you? What is so special about you?"

For most people, this would appear to be a callous question, but this is something you need to resolve right now if you are going to move ahead with your idea.

Why would consumers choose to buy your product and ignore other similar ones in the market? What are the key ingredients you are using that will separate you from the competition?

Most consumers, as well as the fictional venture capitalists above, the price of the product will be a major determining factor. If you can keep your overheads and labor costs down, you will be able to charge less than the competition. However, there is another key ingredient that matters more than anything else. You! Consumers want to be able to relate to the person behind the product. They need to feel that human connection so they can determine whether you are like them or not.

It's great if you build a large company that provides amazing products, but if people can't see you as a friend, they will simply go somewhere else. Even if your product appears plain and boring on the surface, if you can find a way to add a personal element to it, people will connect with it and open up their wallets for you. This is what you can consider your unfair advantage over your competitors.

Now you are beginning to understand why we haven't dived into market research and idea validation yet. You first need to check out how well you connect with your intended audience. You may be saying to yourself that you won't be the public face of the company, but that isn't what we are looking at. We want to determine which aspects of you will be integrated into your business.

Now, one of the venture capitalists had asked you a question, and you still haven't answered it yet.

"Whatever it is you are selling, I can probably pay someone else to do right now. Why do I need to work with you? What is so special about you?"

What kind of answer would you give? Most people would fumble on this one, yet it is something you should be able to answer. Some would quickly launch into presenting a statistical argument as to how large the market is and how special the product is. Yet the truth is that another entrepreneur can swoop in at any time and create something similar and probably better. There goes your unfair advantage!

You may feel fear, self-doubt, and embarrassment creeping into you as you try to answer this question. Do not worry. You are not the only one. Every successful entrepreneur has gone through such a thing. The difference between those who had great ideas but failed and those who succeeded lies in pressing through these emotions. You simply have to set your fear and doubts aside and move forward.

The question being asked by the venture capitalist is direct and simple: What are you bringing to the market that nobody else can bring? In other words, talk to us about your unfair advantage.

Understanding Unfair Advantages
An unfair advantage can be described as an asset or skill you possess that nobody else has. It can be something only a few people have within a specified niche. Consider it a competitive edge that you must learn how to use to create and shape your business.

You may be wondering how this may be any different from your Unique Selling Proposition (USP), which is something entrepreneurs deal with when they are creating their business. Well, a USP is more focused on how different your business is from its competitors. On the other hand, an unfair advantage focuses on you, the entrepreneur. Think of it as a superpower that you can use to make your business more successful.

So back to that one question you seriously need to answer.

What is so special about you?

For a few of you, the answer is already clear, which is great. The majority usually needs some time to seriously think of an answer to this question. If you fall into this second category, you are probably racking your brain right now trying to come up with something. There is no problem if you are struggling with this. Doing this by yourself may be difficult, and you may be surprised that other people can spot this answer for you.

Exercise
We want you to think of ten people that know you well and send them an email asking them to point out your superpowers.

Yes, this may sound a bit weird, but do it anyway. In most cases, you either underestimate your strengths or overestimate your weaknesses, but if you can get an objective opinion from the people around you, it will be possible to get a clearer picture. The only way you can maximize your strengths is if you know what they are.

When it comes to asking people about your weaknesses, things may get a little awkward or emotional. However, in this case, we are only going to focus on your strong points.

You can create a personalized message and copy it to the 10 people you want to help you identify your strengths. Remember that people see things differently, so you may end up with unique answers. However, what you should keep an eye out for are the points of commonality between the different answers.

It is possible you won't get clear answers from your respondents. Though the responses may not be as refined as you expected, at least you have some information to work with as we move further into the book. Never forget that your uniqueness is what will separate you from the rest of the pack and provide that human connection that consumers are seeking.

CHAPTER 5: STICKING TO YOUR MISSION

As we move forward into the other sections of the book, you are going to start to lose sight of the important things that you have learned so far. This also happens after you have established your business.

The point we are trying to make here is that being an entrepreneur consists of long hours working on a project. Somewhere down the road, you are going to start questioning why you are slogging away so much. If you cannot remember why you are doing whatever you are doing, you will find yourself losing motivation and even be tempted to quit.

It is at times like these that you need to remind yourself what you are fighting for. Sticking to your mission is tough, and in business, you are always trying to accomplish one thing so you can move on to the next one. This can sometimes make it hard to focus on the bigger picture.

What drives you to keep going during the hard times? When things get hard, what can you focus on to provide that inner fire to keep you striving for greater success? Is it your kids? Is it money? Is it ambition? Whatever it is, make sure it is something that can remind you of your mission; something that will support your mission and push you forward.

The mission that you are on is a personal journey that belongs to you and you alone. You must always have something that reminds you of what that mission is; otherwise, situations and even people will draw you away from it. This is why you need to keep the sheet of paper from the Future Test. Remember the exercise that involved the four quadrants back in the second chapter? That's the one.

This piece of paper is a representation of what your future looks like. What you wrote down are the things you are striving for. Keep it somewhere visible so you can see it every time you are working towards your goal. When people ask you about it, tell them what it represents to you. This will add extra meaning to what you are doing.

PART II: DEVELOPING YOUR IDEA

It's time to get your hands dirty. In this part of the book, you are going to take the business idea you have, break it down, and then run tests to better understand what you are working with. Items that are unnecessary will be sliced off and your idea will begin to resemble the finished article.

Let's go!

CHAPTER 6: DON'T PUT THE CART BEFORE THE HORSE!

We live in a digital world today where everything can be done online as quick and easy as possible. The rise of the Internet has led to the proliferation of web-based companies, with many young entrepreneurs rushing to set up websites for businesses that aren't even in existence yet.

Many entrepreneurs are creating web pages, printing business cards, and designing logos way before their business idea is even fleshed out. You find so many companies with social media accounts and email addresses yet they don't sell anything to consumers. This is indicative of a person who has gone ahead to put the cart before the horse.

Now, we are not trying to say these things aren't important. It's great to have a business website, logo, and social media account, but these things won't help you until you fully develop your idea. You are trying to brand your business without fully understanding what it does, its target market, and its unique selling proposition.

Why do most entrepreneurs today choose to act this way? The answer is simple: It is fun! You have seen the processes, tests, and exercises we have gone through in the first section of this book. For most people, this probably seemed boring and unpleasant. You were probably wondering when we would get to the juicy, fun part.

On the other hand, designing your own website and creating a cool logo is a fun process every entrepreneur enjoys. Setting up social media accounts and chatting with potential customers is also enjoyable. You literally put in a little effort into these things and are rewarded with instant results, unlike slogging away trying to create a comprehensive business model from an idea.

We all want to see results quickly and with minimal effort. However, the problem with this way of thinking is that you develop a default mode of running to the easy tasks whenever things start becoming difficult. You may have started developing your idea, but somewhere along the way you got stuck, and instead of sticking it out, you looked for something fun to do, like designing your business cards. You tricked yourself into believing you were moving the business forward.

Apart from spending time creating visuals and social media for your business, there is one other thing many entrepreneurs waste time on. This is common during the early phases of the journey. This one thing is naming your business.

Believe it or not, there are people out there who had great business ideas but didn't develop them further simply because they couldn't settle on a good name! On some level, this is understandable. For an entrepreneur, setting up a business is like birthing a baby. You want to raise them well and make sure they have everything they need to grow up big and strong. They will cause you to lose some sleep and even puke all over you, but deep down you recognize they are a blessing. Just like you would never raise your child without a name, you cannot develop a business without a name either. On the other hand, you need to realize that wasting time stressing over a business name eats into the time you should be spending getting your idea out into the market.

You most likely have a name already picked out for your business, and that's cool. A name makes something appear authentic and real, and this can provide you with the motivation you need to keep going. However, you should also realize that whatever name you have picked can still change.

If you haven't settled on a definitive name yet, there's nothing to worry about. Just pick a name that fits your current idea and roll with it. You will change it later on once you have clarified and validated your idea, and identified the target consumer.

We are going to develop your potential business idea through the various exercises coming up in the subsequent chapters. Your mind may contain different elements of your idea, so step one will be to organize your thoughts so you can get a clear vision of what you need. The next step will be to mold the raw materials you have into something that makes more sense. Not to say that what you have is senseless, but, anyway, you get the picture.

Be prepared to discard stuff you thought was important but really isn't. By the time we are done, you will have shaped your idea and added some crucial details that make it worth sharing with others. This will help you gain honest feedback that will propel you into the latter parts of the book.

CHAPTER 7: GERMINATING YOUR IDEA

In this chapter, you are going to engage in the first exercise designed to help you understand the essence of your idea. In other words, we want to see what your idea is all about, not just figuratively but visually as well. Every thought you have ever had regarding your idea will be pieced together as you try to form something real.

Creating Your Mind Map
Though the human brain is a versatile organ, its capacity to focus on multiple things at the same time is extremely limited. In most cases, we fail to arrange our thoughts in the order necessary to make things clear, and this means we are likely to forget a lot of things unless we record the thoughts.

One valuable method of solving this problem is creating a mind map. Mind mapping can be described as forming a visual image that represents your thoughts. This is a skill that all entrepreneurs need to have, as it provides a useful method for organizing thoughts and seeing patterns in your way of thinking. Your head may be full of disjointed thoughts right now, but a mind map can help you piece everything together so you start to see the linkages and hierarchies involved.

The great thing about mind maps is you can practically use them for anything that you are trying to organize.

You can create one for blog post ideas, podcasts, writing a book, designing a room, or new businesses.

The key to making a mind map work is to make sure every thought is typed or written down in a way that makes it easy to move around individual thoughts. It's important to let you know that writing a list, creating a bubble diagram, or typing in an MS Word document just won't cut it. There are two specific techniques that have proved very useful to us, and we recommend them to all entrepreneurs. One of these methods uses the traditional paper and pen routine, while the other is in digital format.

#1: The Post-It Notes Method

This is a great way to gather and organize your thoughts. If you put down every thought on its own Post-It note, you will be able to move around each thought and group them accordingly. This way, you will also find it easier to eliminate individual thoughts.

The different colors make the work fun, and when you want to focus on a single thought, you can pluck it from the mind map and stick it either on your wall or on the computer.

However, there are two challenges to using this method. The first one is the issue of space. A mind map made from Post-It notes can occupy a large space and you may be forced to do away with it sooner or later. The second issue applies to people who have kids in the house. Children love to use these notes as stickers, and if you are not careful, you might find a couple of them missing. It is always best to take a snapshot of your mind map just in case you lose some notes.

#2: Mind Mapping Tools
There are several online mind-mapping software you can use, in case handling small bits of paper isn't your thing. One of the best in the market is MindMeister, and you can start out with a free trial on the website www.mindmeister.com. With a wonderful and simple interface, you can also download the mobile app so that you are able to access your mind map wherever you go.

Using the software is easy and it shouldn't take you long to get the hang of it. The software allows you to drag individual thoughts and drop them anywhere on the screen. You can also group particular thoughts together and create hierarchies. No need to take snapshots here because you can simply save your work for later.

Now that you have learned the two methods of creating mind maps, we will be doing some practical lessons later on. However, there is one specific aspect of effective mind mapping we must point out.

Do Not Think!
Well, this is a weird statement to make, considering we are dealing with thoughts here. How is it possible to gather and arrange your thoughts without thinking?

Let's look at it from a slightly psychological perspective.

When you are in the process of creating something new, your mind will be in either one of two states: creative state or editing state. In the creative state, your mind focuses on imagining and creating new ideas. The editing state is where you become logical and analytical. Majority of people rarely stay in one state for long, and the tendency is to switch from creating to editing and back to creating. This is what happens when someone is writing, say, an email.

The problem with this mental back and forth is that the editing state interferes with your creative process. There are some wonderful ideas that would have popped up but due to your editor mind, they fail to come out. Instead of having a smooth and continuous flow of creative thoughts, your mind starts judging each thought that comes out and tries to make it perfect. This is why you need to stop thinking so you avoid going into the editing state.

When you first start mapping your thoughts during the mind mapping exercise, just dive into creative mode and allow your ideas to flow out onto your screen or notes. Every idea that comes out should be noted down. Don't judge your ideas as either smart or stupid. Just write everything that comes out.

Do Not Think!

Once you are done with allowing all your creative juices to flow, you can then start editing your thoughts. This is where you move thoughts around, arrange them in groups and levels, and get rid of the ones that won't work.

Let's move on to the three stages of the mind mapping exercise.

Stage One: The Open Mind
You will need the following items:
• Your preferred method of creating mind maps (i.e. software or Post-It notes)
• A quiet place to work uninterrupted
• A timer or just your Smartphone; Set for ten minutes
• Anything that relaxes you and stimulates creative thoughts e.g. music, chair
• An open mind

When you have all these items, follow the instructions below. Please read through all the instructions first and then begin the exercise.

1. Start the timer and then quickly write down or type all the thoughts linked to your business idea. Just write what pops into your head and avoid editing or moving at this stage.
2. For those using software, simply create a new branch for every thought you have. For Post-It notes, don't bother sticking them somewhere. Just place them down and keep writing. Don't worry if things look messy.
3. There are times when you will be thinking faster than your fingers can write/type, while other times you will stop and be staring into space. No matter

what happens, just keep writing until the 10 minutes is over.

Stage Two: Clean Up

1. When the 10 minutes is over, you may end up with a mess of notes, either in paper or digital form. Now start editing and organizing.
2. Arrange those thoughts that seem related to one another into groups. You can name the groups using the software or color code the Post-It notes.
3. You may begin to notice there are hierarchies both between and within the groups. If so, start to arrange the thoughts in order.
4. At this stage, you can start analyzing the thoughts as much as you want. You may discover some holes in your thoughts, so if you feel the need to add more thoughts, go ahead. You are now trying to understand your idea on a deeper level.
5. In some cases, some thoughts won't fit any group. This is okay. Just create a group for these wandering thoughts.
6. Your idea started off as a seed but has now developed into a tree of organized thoughts, with branches and leaflets to boot. This shows your idea now has some form of structure to it.

Unfortunately, just like with any tree whose branches and leaves grow wild, you have to do the necessary pruning with your ideas too.

Stage Three: Pruning Time
When it comes to establishing a viable and sustainable business, more may often be a bad idea. You have spent quite some time and effort coming up with great thoughts, but now you have to painfully prune what is not required. You have all the raw materials together, but now it is time to create a proper structure.

You should begin by getting rid of the thoughts that obviously don't belong there. Anything that makes you wonder what was going on in your head should probably be removed. The thoughts that remain are what you need going forward.

Keep in mind there will be more pruning in the future as we define your target consumers and potential competitors. This will happen in the third part of the book. For now, you can leave your mind map as it is.

CHAPTER 8: THE SINGLE SENTENCE

In this chapter, you are going to learn an interesting yet critical tool. You are going to convert your whole mind map into one single sentence. Why is this necessary?

One of the most important tools that can help you get things done faster and more effectively is communication. Not just any kind of communication; the kind of communication that allows you to get to the root of any situation as quickly as possible. When you discover the root of something, you are finally able to figure out what matters the most.

The exercise we are about to engage in involves taking the mind map you created and converting all your thoughts into one sentence. This single sentence is what will allow you to share what your business idea is all about with others. Don't think of it as an elevator pitch for now because you are not yet trying to sell your idea to anyone. We just want to share the idea with others so that you gain honest feedback.

Creating That One Sentence
If anyone were to take a good look at your mind map at this moment, they probably wouldn't understand what you have created. They may be familiar with mind maps, but interpreting all your thoughts would be difficult. You need to see this process as an exercise in translating what you have created into an understandable language.

There are three steps in translating your ideas. Each step helps you refine your idea further and break it down into its core elements.

Step One: Writing a Single Page
First of all, you will summarize your mind map in one page of fewer than 500 words. You have the freedom to write as you wish according to what you have in your mind map. Don't even worry about grammar at this point. Just have fun.

Step Two: Writing a Single Paragraph
Now you have to summarize that one page you wrote and compress it into a single paragraph of about 5 sentences. Think of the information that an interested party might need to know about your idea. This may be a bit difficult to do, but keep working on it. Write and refine as many times as possible until you end up with 5 sentences that clearly describe what your business is about.

Step Three: Writing a Single Sentence
In this last step, summarize what you wrote in 5 sentences and create a single sentence. This step doesn't require a lot of writing, but it will definitely take you longer than the rest. You may find yourself writing different versions of the same sentence until you discover the one you prefer.

Read the sentence loudly. How does it sound and feel? Make sure it excites you and invokes some passion because if it doesn't, the people you share it with will also be apathetic toward your idea. In the final chapter of this section of the book, you are going to be confidently sharing your one sentence with others.

CHAPTER 9: SHARING AND OBSERVING YOUR IDEA

During the course of writing this book, we talked to a number of seasoned entrepreneurs who had experience building successful businesses from scratch. In one of our conversations, we started discussing strategies and best practices that a budding entrepreneur can use to succeed. In other words, what were some of those first steps that an entrepreneur needs to follow the moment they come up with a business idea? In all honesty, the answer we got was totally unexpected. To put it simply, this is what we learned:

One of the first things you must do when you get an amazing idea is put it down on a piece of paper. Most people just keep their ideas in their head, but writing it down helps you flesh out the idea as much as possible. It would be great if you can type it and save it on an app like Evernote or a Word document, but there is something special that happens when you place your idea onto paper. Just grab a pen and paper and jot down the idea.

The next step is to put that piece of paper in your pocket or bag and carry it everywhere for a few weeks, or maybe even a month. Tell everybody about your new idea, starting with those people closest to you. Share it with your spouse, kids, friends, colleagues, and even strangers you meet in the Supermarket. Everyone actually means EVERYBODY.

Why is this so important? As you begin to share your idea with more people, you begin to refine it, and the idea matures.

Some of the feedback may be positive but expect some instant negative feedback as well. There are people out there who will think you are stupid or crazy, but this is actually a good thing. This is your opportunity to whip out that paper and note down the thoughts of others, both positive and negative. The more you do this, the better your idea gets.

Now, most of you are probably asking one critical question. What if somebody steals my idea?

The truth is that there is nothing preventing somebody from copying your idea. However, there is one thing that you probably haven't considered: Your inner passion and commitment to bring your idea to life! You see, there are millions of million-dollar ideas floating around in people's minds, but few of them are ever executed. In other words, it doesn't matter if someone tries to copy your idea. The differentiating factor will always be that you are willing to make sacrifices to execute the idea and the majority of people are not.

You should also consider the fact that you have an unfair advantage, which we talked about earlier in the book. So what if someone tries to copy your idea? You just need to figure out your unfair advantage and all will be well. There is something that only you have and potential competitors don't, so don't let this fear hold you back from sharing your idea.

You have to start talking about your idea before you execute it. As you get more feedback from others, your motivation levels also rise, and you get more excited about it every day. You gradually build momentum, and as time goes by, your idea matures from good to great.

Another aspect of sharing your idea is that people will be willing to give you some new or sometimes even better ideas than the one you had. This shows you the power of sharing your ideas and observing them as they evolve into something more than what you were expecting.

Dealing with Negative Feedback
We have seen how talking about your idea can make it massively better. Since this will probably be the first time you are going public with your business idea, there are some critical things that we need to discuss first.

Most people get nervous when it comes to sharing their ideas, and understandably so. It is not an easy thing to do, considering there are people out there who enjoy eviscerating other people's ideas. You need to learn how to take criticism well because, for sure, you will meet people who will give negative feedback.

The challenge that most budding entrepreneurs have is balancing the positive and negative comments. For some reason, we have a huge problem doing math when it comes to feedback. You can get hundreds of positive comments, but that one negative comment is what your mind will latch onto for the whole day. It can be especially gut wrenching when that one negative comment was said in a disrespectful manner.

As an entrepreneur, you have to learn how to tune out negative feedback that is aimed at being disrespectful. Negative feedback is good if it is meant to help you refine your idea and improve customer experience, but do not waste time thinking about what haters and trolls say about your idea. Take what is useful for improving your idea and ignore the rest.

At the end of the day, being an entrepreneur requires having a thick skin. You can't live without haters, so just get used to receiving negative feedback once in a while. It will definitely make you a better entrepreneur in the long run.

Exercise
Take the business idea you have and tell it to 10 different people over the next 2 days. It would be great if you can talk to more than 10 people, but this is a good number to start with.

Of course, you should begin with people whom you are comfortable with. Start with those who care about you and are willing to listen to your idea. After that, you can find at least 2 strangers and discuss your idea with them.

Remember that your whole target idea has been condensed into one sentence, so it is now easier to articulate it clearly and quickly. Here are some more tips to help you during this challenge.

Tips for Sharing Your Idea:
1. Avoid offering your opinion when starting the conversation. You will be tempted to begin conversations by saying things like, "Check out this cool idea...." or "Listen to this awesome idea I came up with." The problem with opening with such statements is that it frames your idea in a particular way, yet we want the idea to speak for itself. We want honest, unbiased, feedback.

2. Don't talk negatively about yourself or the idea. Most people have this annoying tendency to make excuses when pitching their idea. This is when you open conversations by saying your idea isn't fully complete yet or you didn't have adequate time to think it through. If your opening statement about your idea is negative, how do you expect a positive response from people? Just be confident and refuse to make excuses.

3. Offer some help first and then ask for a favor. This is helpful advice when trying to talk to strangers about your idea. Your approach should be to offer a person your help first, for example, buying them a coffee if you happen to be in line at Starbucks. This provides you with a way to initiate a conversation. Just ask them to spare a minute to listen to your idea. Even if they say they don't have the time, it's okay. However,

since you have done them a favor, they are likely to return it by giving you feedback.

Tips on Listening to Feedback
1. Listen consciously to their feedback. The moment the other person starts responding, your brain will begin to wander. You need to make sure you listen well so you don't miss any important feedback that might improve your idea.

2. Avoid recording the conversation. Most people get nervous when faced with a recording device or notepad, and they might respond by telling you what they think you want to hear rather than their honest opinion.

3. Don't interrupt them. Allow people the time to respond adequately to your idea.

4. Ask short follow-up questions to gain a deeper perspective. Once the person finishes giving their opinion, ask them some questions to gain a deeper insight. For example, "Why do you feel that is important?" "What else is missing?" and etc.

5. Watch their non-verbal signals. It's not just about what the person says. You also have to read their vocal signals and body language. Do they sound excited or bored by the idea?

Once a conversation is over, you should immediately write down or record the feedback.

Wow! You have come a long way, haven't you? Your idea is beginning to take shape, and you've gained vital feedback. Take another look at the mind map you created and see if you can add any new ideas from the feedback received. Your original idea may change somewhat, and it may be a good idea to go back and share your refined idea with people to gain more feedback.

You should also keep in mind that just because you gained a lot of positive responses doesn't automatically mean the business will be successful. The target customer may respond differently from the people you talked to. This is why we take you through some tests later on so the target consumers can validate your idea.

Let's move on to the third part of the book!

PART III: CHECKING OUT YOUR BUSINESS ENVIRONMENT

In this part of the book, we are going to determine who your target customer is, where we can find them, and their preferred means of engagement. We shall also perform some examinations to identify potential partners and competitors in the market.

CHAPTER 10: IDENTIFYING YOUR CORE AUDIENCE

In the world of entrepreneurship, you will experience the pressure to cater to as large a market as possible. You will look around you and see what everybody else is doing, and be tempted to follow the crowd. Most people believe in the saying, "Go big or go home," yet for a new entrepreneur, this may be a daunting task for their new business.

Sure, it is great to want to reach as large an audience as possible with your business. We all want to change the world in one way or another, touch the lives of millions, or create the next big thing. Merely making money on a monthly basis is never part of any entrepreneur's plans.

So the question then becomes, "Are you thinking too small?"

This is the way we want you to see things.

Building a successful business should never be just about the money. It should be based on helping people. There is a strong tendency to come up with a product that will be accepted by and change the lives of millions, but what if you could simply focus on a small group of customers and get them to fall in love with your product? It may not change the whole world but it will definitely change the world of your niche market.

Being ambitious and wanting to be the next Facebook is cool, but what we want you to learn from this book is that success can be achieved without having to market to the whole world. All you have to do is create a core fan base that will see your business as vital to their lives. Targeting millions of customers from the get-go can be debilitating for a new entrepreneur, and even getting people's attention can be difficult at first.

One of the most powerful pieces of business advice comes from Kevin Kelly of Wired Magazine. He wrote an article explaining how success can be achieved by simply acquiring 1000 genuine fans rather than trying to make your idea go viral. So what exactly defines a genuine fan? This is the kind of person who will buy every product your business produces. They will listen to all your podcasts, come to all your shows, watch all your videos, and read all your blog posts. They will support your business because they love what you offer them.

What is the point we are trying to make here?

We live in a world of over seven billion individuals, yet underneath this large population, there are many diverse sub-groups you can cater for. You don't need to target everyone out there to become a successful entrepreneur. All you have to do is find those true fans whose lives you can change through your product or service.

So, should you be thinking small? No, just think small enough to change the lives of your core fan base.

Find Your Niche
By now you should have realized there is great potential to make money if you can only find your niche market. What you need to do is conduct proper research to unearth those sub-groups that comprise people with similar problems, habits, and needs. Once you find this niche, narrow it down as much as possible so you can provide better service. It is easier to cater for the interests of and connect with a small homogenous group than trying to satisfy everyone.

Don't worry about how you are going to do this. We are with you every step of the way. Let's flip over to the next chapter, where we will learn how to research your target market and identify customers as well as existing competitors.

CHAPTER 11: MAPPING YOUR MARKET

We may have a good enough understanding of what your business idea is, but at this point, we still don't know much about where your audience is located, who currently serves them, and the products they prefer. This chapter is going to help us map out your market so you have a better perspective of what you are getting into. This will also enable you to maneuver confidently through the market as you start and nurture your business.

As we start researching the market, you need to know there are potentially other businesses that may be producing a similar product or service as your own. This is not meant to discourage you. Many potential entrepreneurs have chosen not to start their businesses due to the presence of other similar ideas in the market. Don't allow fear to prevent you from achieving your dreams.

Consider it a plus if there are already competitors serving the same niche you are targeting. At least you will be able to learn from their mistakes and successes and design your business model appropriately. After that, your job will be to differentiate your business from the rest so that you are able to stand out. Instead of making better products, focus on being different in the way you serve your customers.

Developing a Market Map
There are three distinct aspects of your market you must look at. These are:

- Places
- People
- Products

Create a spreadsheet for each of these elements, then create three columns in each spreadsheet. The columns should be named Name, Web Address, and Notes. We suggest you create a master file and set up Places, People, and Products as sub-sheets. This master file will also come in handy as you will be creating other sheets later on. You can use MS Excel, Numbers for Mac, or for easier access, Google Drive.

Places
One critical factor for every business, including offline ones, is to discover where their online audience is located. As you conduct this research, you will come across websites that cater to your target audience, thus giving you an opportunity to know who these people are. For example, you can find forums where users talk about certain products. You can use these forums to advertise your business as well as share articles to build trust within the market.

One of the best ways to find places of interest for your intended audience is Google, so let's see what we can find.

1. Blogs

We can quickly Google for the best blogs within the niche you are targeting. Blogs can provide you with access to communities where users normally interact. You can discover the issues users are concerned about and what's hot in the market.

Since there are probably thousands of blogs that deal with a particular niche, you need to find a way to cut through the noise and get what you want. You should start by going to the Google search box and typing in:

blog: keyword

Keep in mind that keyword here represents the topic you are searching for, For example, if your business idea is related to the fast food industry, you will type;

blog: fast food

The first page that comes up contains the most relevant blogs. You can also click on the options provided at the bottom of the page showing the search items related to your keyword.

With only a single keyword, you can find hundreds of blogs linked to whatever topic you are interested in. However, there are certain niches that aren't compatible with blogging, so if your keyword doesn't generate blog results, you should consider using a different keyword related to your target market and audience. If this also fails, just move on to forums instead.

At this point, you should be able to fill in the three columns in your Places spreadsheet. You have the name of relevant blogs, their web addresses (which should be clickable for faster access), and any special information you feel may come in handy later.

2. Forums
Forums also provide a lot of great information, especially because it is the audience who generates the conversations rather than the owner of the website. When using Google, the procedure is the same as before. In the search box, just type:

forum: fast food

Forums are not as prolific as blogs, so try to get the ones within the first page of your results. Fill in your spreadsheet the same way you did with the blogs.

3. Social Media
There are many social media groups where your potential audience meets to discuss various topics related to what you are selling. Tapping into this huge resource is one unique way of researching your audience.

You can use any social media platform to conduct your consumer research, but we recommend LinkedIn and Facebook because they have the most relevant groups. Of course, this will depend on the type of business you are engaged in. For example, if you are selling toys, you are better off using Facebook than LinkedIn.

Searching for these groups is easy. All you have to do is log in to your page and type your keyword into the search box at the top of the page. Since you are looking for groups, you may need to click on the tab "More" and you will get a list of relevant groups. If a Facebook group is Public, you can access it immediately, but if it is Private, you will have to request approval from the administrator.

Look at the groups that are most relevant to your business in terms of the number of members, activity levels, and user engagement. Ignore groups that have not had any conversations recently. There's no point wasting time with a group that won't provide you with relevant if any, information. Try to come up with a minimum of 25 groups and note them down in your spreadsheet.

That's it for the Places that can help you develop your map market. Now we are going to use slightly different strategies to find the top influencers in your industry.

People
Locating your audience is one thing, but knowing who your potential competitors are is a whole different ball game. If you are able to identify the people or organizations already serving your target customers, you can gather vital information. You will be able to know what your potential customers like and dislike.

By studying the top influencers in the market, you can learn their strategies, and then decide which people you could form a working relationship with in the future. This information will also help you determine what you need to do to distinguish yourself from the competition.

So how do you keep tabs on the people in your market? You can subscribe to their newsletters via email, and as you study their marketing strategies, you will notice useful patterns. You will see the way they communicate to their audience and spot some of the mistakes they make. This process is not just about learning what to do. It also involves learning what to AVOID.

Finding Top Influencers
Before you start subscribing to newsletters, you first have to find these top influencers. Social media is a great place to start.

Let's use Twitter as an example. Every niche has top influencers, and these people usually have a large number of followers. This indicates the level of authority they have in that niche. In fact, once you start your business, you should prioritize using Twitter to market your brand since it is one of the best platforms for quickly gaining a large audience.

You can use Twitter's advanced search feature to find as many influential people as possible, depending on the primary keyword you use. You can narrow down the search results using the parameters available. Just make sure you are dealing with top and active accounts. The great thing about Twitter is they make it so easy to run these searches thanks to their advanced ranking algorithm.

Don't be surprised if you find accounts with smaller numbers of followers being ranked as top influencers. In fact, it may be easier to build a relationship with people who have smaller yet more active groups. We recommend you collect about 20 accounts and feed them into your spreadsheet.

Apart from Twitter, you can also use other social media platforms such as Facebook, LinkedIn, Instagram, and Periscope. There are also search engines that can come in handy when trying to find the movers and shakers within a given niche. These include YouTube, iTunes, and BuzzSumo.

Products
We have identified the places where your target audience hangs out and the people who influence them. Now we are going to focus on the products and services that your audience needs.

Why is this necessary? If you can identify what the audience is buying right now, you will be able to know what is on offer in the market, and what is not. If people are willing to open their wallets to buy a product, it means they are getting their money's worth. You should also know that just because a website says that a product is one of their best-selling products; it doesn't mean real people are purchasing it. Take the time to look for other products that may not be selling as much, just to get a feel for what is out there.

So where do we start? Well, Amazon.com is a great product website. It is actually a search engine that allows you to browse through thousands of different products and services from a wide variety of niches.

Type your keyword into the search box and you will get results based on the popularity of a product. Note down the relevant products in your spreadsheet as well as their web links. In the Notes section, you can include the product rating, reviews, and price point.

By now you realize that you have a treasure trove of about a hundred names and web addresses of Places, People, and Products. You may be worried about how everything will fit together, but we'll get to that later on. We will show you how to dig deeper through all the data we have gathered so far, and what conclusions we can make regarding your target audience.

CHAPTER 12: UNDERSTANDING YOUR CUSTOMER

You have spent a lot of time and energy learning about your market, your target customers, the major influencers in your niche, and the products available. Great job! It may seem like too much work, but you need to understand that the research you are doing will help you achieve success much faster than those entrepreneurs who launched without a plan. All you have to do is take action.

Most entrepreneurs believe that creating a successful business is all about them, but the truth is that it is not. It's about serving the needs of your customers. This will only be possible if you know who your customer is, what they want, and how to get them to pay for it.

You may be asking yourself why you didn't start the book off by learning about the customer. If serving the needs of customers is the most important thing, isn't that what you should have started with?

That may be the common way of doing a business, but we took a different approach for a reason. For people who don't have any clue about what type of business to start, it would have been logical to start by looking at what the market needs. However, the problem with this approach is that you may end up with a great business idea that you aren't interested in. You may start strong, but your motivation will soon fade away.

On the other hand, we know you picked up this book already having one or several ideas in mind. It was just an issue of picking the one to focus on. This is where most budding entrepreneurs get stuck. Once we ran your idea through a couple of tests, we were able to refine it, and ultimately, you became more assured that your idea was in a niche that you are genuinely passionate about. You now understand what you prefer and all that remains is finding the right customers to move your business forward.

Makes sense, doesn't it?

Now, in order to help you understand your target customer, we want to introduce a strategy guide referred to as Customer PLAN. This stands for customer:

1. P - Problems
2. L- Language
3. A- Anecdotes
4. N- Needs

What you need to do right now is open your master spreadsheet and add a new sub-sheet titled PLAN. Within the sub-sheet, create four columns and name them after the four PLAN elements mentioned above.

1. Problems
Every business idea you have should be targeted at solving your customer's problems. You find the

problem, you solve it, and you get paid. Everything else is secondary.

There are three ways of finding out the problems your customers are facing. These are real-time conversations, surveys, and paid traffic.

Real-Time Conversations
Sending your target audience emails may be the popular thing to do, but the best way is actually speaking to them in person or picking up the phone and calling them. Unlike the exercise where we asked you to share your target idea with others, this time you are dealing with customers, so asking the right questions is a necessity.

Some of the questions you can ask include:
• Your customer's frustrations
• The changes they would like to see to a product/service
• The challenges costing them a lot of money
• The things that consume their most time
• The current solutions they use to solve their problems

Don't be afraid to dig deeper and ask follow-up questions. Use the spreadsheet you created and go to the Places where your customers hang out online. Get acquainted with people and ask them for their phone number or chat on Skype. You can also attend relevant conventions and events to talk to people in person.

Surveys

This should be your second option in case you cannot manage to have personal conversations with target customers. Surveys enable you to gather vital data as quickly as possible.

In the same way that real-time conversations require you to ask pertinent questions, an effective survey must also include questions that reveal the challenges that customers endure. When conducting your survey, ask your target customers the biggest problem that they face regarding product/service/idea X.

This question may seem too simple, but it is powerful because it is an open question that allows customers to tell their stories and struggles. You also need to recognize the kind of language the customer uses in their response, as this may come in handy when creating promotional material.

Do you already have an email list of customers or followers on social media? If so, send them this one question, making sure to provide a context for asking for their help. To ensure more genuine responses, don't elaborate too much about why you are asking the question.

In case you do not have an email list or social media following, there are still ways of conducting your survey. You could visit the websites or social media accounts of the target customers and ask them whether they would like to participate in a survey.

This is the time to use the information we collected in the master spreadsheet.

Paid Traffic
If all else fails, you may have to use an advertising platform to drive traffic to a web page and then survey them there. This is possible by paying for Facebook or Twitter adverts, but you can also use Google AdWords.

Finally, and most importantly, don't forget to fill in customer problems into the PLAN spreadsheet.

2. Language
As an entrepreneur, it is crucial to learn your customers' language and communication style. How do they express their problems and desires? If you can bridge the communication gap, you will find it easier to establish a human connection and gain their trust.

There are three distinct elements of your target customer's language: Questions, Complaints, and Keywords.

Questions
In this section, we are interested in knowing the exact questions being asked by customers. How do we do this?

Remember the forums we recorded in the Market Map spreadsheet? Go back to the spreadsheet and pick the web address of one of the forums. Copy and paste it into the Google search bar, then add the words "how do I" at the front, like this:

"how do I" site: www.thenextbigthing.com

This will enable you to search through the forum abcdefg.com for any instances where people have used "how do I" to inquire for help. By the way, the quotation marks are very important because they inform the search engine that the words must appear in that exact order. There are many other words you can use, such as "Please help," "how can I," "I need," and etc.

Another way of accessing target customers' questions is the FAQs page of a website. The process is pretty much the same as before. You can use Google to find the FAQ page of a specific blog as shown below:

"faq" site: www.thenextbigthing.com

Note down any questions that appear relevant into your spreadsheet, both from the forums and FAQ page.

Complaints
When customers complain, they tend to use emotional language, and this can help you become more empathetic and relate better to their needs. There are two ways of finding customer complaints. You can perform a forum search as we did before with the questions, except this time you will use complaining words. For example:

"I hate" site: www.thenextbigthing.com

The second way of getting complaints is using Amazon Reviews. This is a simple and a straightforward process. Just go to Amazon and look for one of the products you recorded in your Market Map spreadsheet. Scroll down to the reviews section and focus on the 3- and 2-star ratings. These are the guys who actually spent money on the product and are giving their honest feedback. They won't mind going into details. The problem with the 1-star and 5-star reviews are that they could be from either business rivals or friends of the owner of the product. Record these complaints in your spreadsheet. You will need them later on.

Keywords
This is the last element of a customer's language. Keywords are the words people type into a search engine when they are looking for something. If you can determine the keywords constantly being used by customers, you will be able to design your content and advertising around them.

To get your relevant keywords, use any keyword that is related to your niche and type it into Google's search bar. After you press Enter, scroll down the results page and look at the other related keywords in "Searches Related To" area. Type them into your spreadsheet.

We recommend you get long-tail keywords for more effective results, so click on one of the links at the bottom of the page. This will open up a new results page. Scroll to the bottom and you will find a new list of long-tail keywords. Record these in your spreadsheet. If you want, you can keep clicking through these links to find more keywords.

3. Anecdotes
These are short stories that are used to highlight a particular issue. For example, a customer may share an experience they had when using a particular product. Anecdotes usually contain details and lessons to be learned, and they enable one person to share their memories with others.

Everyone loves a good story, and it's a great way to get people's attention. The goal of this section is to help you find real customer stories that will help you connect with customers and their experiences. By reading or hearing stories from real-life people, you are more likely to base your business decisions on solving real-life problems.

One of the best ways to get anecdotes is by talking to people in person. If you can meet your target customers personally, you should ask them to narrate stories about their problems and pains.

These stories are also available online and all you have to do is know where to find them. You can use the forums you recorded in your spreadsheet. Use the same tactic as before, where we placed a keyword in front of the web address and searched it using Google. For example:

"awesome story" site: www.thenextbigthing.com

Try to use as many different keyword search terms as possible to find great stories to use as anecdotes.

You can also listen to podcast interviews, though these can be more difficult to come by compared to forums. You get to listen to a person's story as they narrate it in a conversation with the interviewer. To find an anecdote in a podcast, you can use Google again. In the search bar, type in the word "podcast" followed by the relevant keywords. For example:

Podcast "story about" "kite design"

As you read and listen to people's stories, you will feel more confident about providing a solution to their problems. You will feel what they feel, and this will now help you to move to the next step where we determine the diverse needs of your target audience.

4. Needs
This is where we close the PLAN. You have now understood the target market, and what is left is to compile a list of customer needs. Don't get confused about the needs of the customer because most new entrepreneurs assume it is the same thing as the product they want to sell. Needs are the things that are required by customers to solve their problems. The product you are selling is merely a mechanism for solving that problem.

For example, many amateur fly fishermen find it difficult to re-tie their flies fast enough after losing them or whenever they want to switch to another one. After a few one-on-one conversations with them, you discover that the actual problem is that by the time they finish tying the fly, they have missed the chance of catching fish that were in the perfect spot.

In this example, we have two needs:

- The need for improved skills for tying flies.
- The need for quick access to flies.

You can create a business around both these needs! This is what having a PLAN is truly about.

Whatever your original business idea was, it may have transformed into something else entirely by now. Maybe you have decided to move in a totally different direction. Your idea could still be the same. Whatever the case, once you identify the needs of your customers, you will know that you are on the right track.

Exercise
It is now time to engage in a small exercise. Go to your PLAN spreadsheet and "hide" the columns for Language and Anecdotes. Just right-click the header for the two columns, and then select "Hide Column." You are now left with only two columns – Problems and Needs.

The goal is to use each problem that you recorded and try to derive a need from them. Make sure that you move down the list gradually, focusing on a single problem and its potential solutions.

If you cannot find a need to correspond with a problem, don't sweat it. Just keep moving down the list of problems. Take your time to think clearly about what your target audience needs to solve their problems.

At the end of it all, you will have so much information to work with, and in the final part of the book, we will be using all this research to develop a product you're your customers will love!

CHAPTER 13: SOLVING PROBLEMS

As an entrepreneur, your main role is to go into the market, diagnose problems, and develop products or services that solve particular problems. Businesses are meant to provide solutions, and though sometimes you may have to come up with new stuff, often what is required is combining and rearranging existing resources.

By focusing on what the customer needs rather than your own, you will be able to build a business that people will stay loyal to. Better yet, your customers will spread the word to others who may be having similar needs.

The next stage of the process is to incorporate the solutions for the problems and needs diagnosed earlier into your PLAN. Each potential solution will then be tested to validate it.

Let's start by going to the master spreadsheet you created. Open the PLAN sub-sheet and create a column titled Solutions. Move down the list of problems and needs, one at a time, and think of the best solution for each. Depending on the problem and need, you could come up with a product, service, tool, or some kind of software that provides a solution. Don't disqualify ideas just because they sound silly. Just let them flow out.

Once you have filled out your spreadsheet with a number of potential solutions, it is time to run some tests. Choose one solution from the group for testing. The great thing about the position you are in is that not only are you going to pick a solution that satisfies customers needs, you are guaranteed of ending up with an idea that fits your life. See how all those exercises in the beginning of the book are beneficial?

The process of picking one solution out of the many you have noted down may be daunting, but there is a way out. Look at your potential solutions and eliminate the ones that don't stir your interest. Instead of deleting, just shade them a different color in case you need to take a second look at them.

It is possible that the idea you started out with isn't on the list, and that is okay. The whole process you have gone through was meant to weed out ideas that didn't deserve your time.

What you need to do next is take your preferred solution and test it the same way we did with your original idea in the beginning of the book. Just follow the steps below:

1. Make sure you pick one problem and the corresponding solution.

2. Think about that solution for 24 hours, jotting down how you feel about it in a notepad. Record any thoughts you have about the solution.

3. Perform the mind-mapping test again, this time using your new solution. Brainstorm for about 10 minutes and then eliminate ideas that don't support your target solution.

4. Write down one page describing your solution, and then summarize this into one paragraph, and finally one sentence.

There's a step that involves sharing your idea with others, but that will be done later on. We are going to use the target customers to tell us whether the idea is viable or not.

Congratulations! You have come a long way and have done work that most entrepreneurs are afraid to do. Many people drop out along the way, but we are glad that you stuck it out.

Let's move on to the final part of the book where we now put your idea to the final test.

PART IV: WILL YOUR DREAM FLY?

In this fourth and final part, we want to see whether the solution you have come up with will pass the flight test. Will your target customer buy the product? Let's find out!

CHAPTER 14: VALIDATING YOUR SOLUTION

Why is the process of validating your idea so important? You could easily just make the product and launch it into the market right now, considering all the work you've put in. The customers have already told us their needs and we have solved their problems, so why waste time with validation?

If there is one critical lesson that every entrepreneur should learn, it is this: there is a huge difference between a customer saying they will buy your product and them actually buying it. You cannot build a sustainable and successful business based on verbal promises. You have to know for sure people will take action and do what they say.

You see, actions speak louder than words. As much as it is important to listen to what others are saying, you have to focus on your numbers. Are people stepping up to buy the product? How many sales have you made? What we are talking about here is almost like developing a few units of your product and then releasing them in order to test how the market responds. This is also referred to as "pre-build" validation.

You are probably wondering if there is a strategy that gives you a 100% guarantee your idea will succeed. Unfortunately, there isn't. There are simply too many variables in the mix, and the only way would be to create the product and see if it sells.

Our goal here is to validate the potential of your idea becoming successful. If the idea works, you will have a lot of motivation to convert this test run into a full-fledged business. On the other hand, if the idea is not successfully validated, at least you will have gained some understanding as to why customers didn't respond positively. This information will help you in redesigning your idea and making it better.

Here are some other benefits of validating your idea:

1. You gain vital feedback from the actions of your target customers. If they buy into your idea, great! If you fail to sell even a single product, you still get the opportunity to know what doesn't work and change a few things.

2. You gain confidence when you sell a few units of your product. This gives you the momentum you will need later on when you finally launch the business.

3. You begin to generate income even before you launch your idea. This will provide cash for paying for the development of your idea.

4. When you see customers responding positively to your idea from the get-go, you are motivated to work harder to deliver what they want. You are more likely to persevere through the hard times if you already know there is a demand for your idea within the target market.

Now that you are convinced of the benefits of validating your idea, let's go into the validation process itself.

CHAPTER 15: HOW TO VALIDATE YOUR IDEA

Validation works when there is action and not just words. There are four steps in the validation process:

1. Stand in Front of An Audience

The validation happens through your target audience, but what happens if you do not already have an email list or a considerable following on social media? There are a number of ways of getting access to audiences:

- **Targeted Advertising** – You can use social media advertising platforms to access people. Google AdWords is also another way to advertise your products. The ads can lead people to your landing page or a survey page. Once you post your ads, you will watch out for the number of clicks, and you will be charged a fee for each click. If nobody clicks on your ad, you won't be required to pay anything, but that also means your ad isn't resonating with the audience. Keep in mind that having many clicks doesn't mean your idea is validated, but rather the ad itself is validated. The actual validation will come later on.

- **Targeted Advertising on Private Sites** – This is where you make an agreement with the owner of a private website to advertise your product or service on their platform. The good thing with this idea is you already know that the site attracts your target audience, so you are piggybacking on an authoritative website to validate your idea. Of course, you will have to part with some cash, but a private site will help you hone in on an existing target market. Clueless about where to find such websites? No worries! Remember the master spreadsheet in Chapter 11 that contains your Market Map? Open up the Places and People sub-sheets and you will find potential websites that already contain your target customers. Strike up a conversation and be honest about what you are asking for.

- **Guest Posting** – You can decide to write an article and publish it on someone else's website. It is a way of getting endorsed by the website owner so their audience can identify you and what you offer. This may be free, but you must have a good relationship with the owner for them to allow you to publish on their site. As before, you can find potential websites in your Market Map spreadsheet.

- **Forums** – The Market Map is going to come in handy again! Go to the Places spreadsheet and look at the forums you recorded. Instead of posting an article on someone else's website, you can simply join a forum and start a conversation. Just be careful you don't make it too obvious you are selling something. Forum members can be hostile when someone new starts advertising their business in their online community. Provide value for a week or two, respond to questions asked, and then start posting your business information. Sign up to about three different forums and identify individuals you can start conversations with.

- **Social Media Groups** – You can find your target audience in LinkedIn and Facebook groups. You can join a community and start building relationships by engaging in active conversations. We recommend you pick three groups that you can participate in every day for one week. Share interesting stuff and post valuable content. As you do this, people will trust you and you can then start asking for favors.

- **Offline Audiences** – While it's more convenient to target online audiences, you should also consider gaining access to live audiences. If you are aware of an event where your audience usually attends, try to get a speaking engagement there. You can start off speaking for free just to build trust and gain experience. There are some conferences that allow people to send in applications to speak about interesting ideas. If this isn't your thing, you could also meet people outside the presentation halls and network with your potential audience.

2. **Hyper Focus Target**
Now that you have understood some of the ways of getting access to your target audience, the next step is hyper-targeting. In other words, you want to convince a section of people they have a need that only your idea can solve. Why only a section? Because it is unlikely that everyone within your target market will be interested in what you have to offer. Instead of trying to target everyone, just focus on those people whose needs match your solution.

For example, if you want to target kids as a toy manufacturer, you won't try to sell your product to everyone between the ages of 0 to 12. Depending on your product, you are going to target a specific age range, and then progressively narrow it down according to other factors. The aim is to find that group of people who will find your solution useful.

So how do you hyper-target a section of your audience? First, you need to ask a question or create a scenario that allows people to show whether they are interested or not. You can post something in a blog, forum, or on social media and watch out for people's responses. You could also watch for the number of clicks on an article or advert you have posted.

Secondly, you can offer a download or ask people to subscribe to your content. You will be able to gauge the audience's interest by the number of subscribers or downloads.

3. **Engage in Active Interactions**
Once you know who to target, the next step is to look for a way to directly interact with these prospects. You need to become comfortable talking to people and making your pitch. The sooner you learn this skill the better. A few people may turn you down but at least you will have gained vital information about why they were not interested. This is information you can use later on.

Sharing your solution with your target audience can be risky because you don't want to seem like you are just asking for money. However, if you know your product can help people, you need to have the confidence to strike conversations, understanding full well that money will change hands down the road. Remember, you are offering value to your customer, not begging for a handout.

So what are some of the ways to go about this? Direct and active interactions require meeting or talking to people in person. These include face-to-face, video calls, phone calls, social media forums, and direct emails. If you already have a large following and want to talk to multiple people at once, you can use a webinar, email broadcast, explainer video, or web article.

Regardless of which method you decide to use, there are three key actions you need to take prior to presenting your solution. These actions will help you build trust and likeability with your audience. They are:

- **Ask them questions to gain more information about them**. The goal is to learn more about your audience and also make them feel comfortable opening up to you. If you are using a webinar, make sure you have live chat enabled. Start off conversations with a greeting and then ask them to talk about what they do for a living. Ask them what made them interested in your product. If you ask the right questions, use the right language, and do a bit of digging before your meeting, you will be able to build rapport quickly.

- **Share information about yourself and why you can help them with their problems and needs.**

- **Keep things honest by being upfront about the reason for the conversation.** If it's feedback you are looking for, let them know from the start. Tell them you have something that can meet their needs and are trying to gauge their interest. This creates trust and allows them the time to think about how relevant your solution is in their lives, even as the conversation carries on.

Remember that you are trying to sell your solution to a potential audience, so you will be relying heavily on your mind map as well as your one sentence. It would be an added advantage if you were to have some sort of prototype to show your customers. Of course, this will be difficult if you are not communicating face-to-face, but at least you should have something that makes your solution more real.

A prototype does not have to be a physical item. It can be a digital item or even a service that you can share with your audience. You can use a model, drawing, outline, or 3D rendering. This prototype is not the finished product, so don't be afraid to show it to people. Assure them that there will be a lot of modifications based on the feedback they give you.

So how will you know whether your solution is a success?

So far, we have been receiving verbal feedback from customers. It is still a bit difficult to say whether they will buy it if you launch the idea. On the flip side, if it sucks, you will definitely know it from the responses you receive.

In the final step of validation, which we are embarking on next, we will be asking those customers who liked the product to cough up some cash. That's right; we will be requesting them to part with their hard earned money even before you develop the final product itself. At a time like this, how you pitch the solution will make the difference between success and failure.

4. Make the Sale

Most new entrepreneurs may feel a bit uncomfortable at this stage. Making the sale here refers to asking your prospect for money yet you haven't built anything yet. However, this should not worry you too much. There are a lot of people who buy into ideas even before seeing the finished product. Platforms such as Indiegogo and Kickstarter are examples of this. You have their attention, shared your plan, and showed them how you will provide value. It is obvious that your prospects validate their interest by agreeing to a sale.

If it's a webinar with multiple attendees, for example, you can provide your web address for them to send their payments. If you are meeting prospects in person, you should do a follow-up 24 hours later and ask them to pre-order. Don't give up in case you don't receive a response within a day. Just send an email to confirm whether they received your first message.

Here are few concerns that you may have about making the sale:

a) **Actual payments versus pre-orders** – Both these options will work since the prospect still has to fill in their payment details. However, customers will feel more secure with a pre-order because money won't be released until they receive the product. Receiving money upfront is great if you need the cash to develop the product, but if you fail to keep your promise, you will have to return the cash.

b) **Optimal pricing** – The price of your product should be considered carefully, but since this is an early release, you should consider offering prospects a big discount. Look at how your competitors are pricing similar products. At this stage, we aren't thinking about profits, but rather validating your business. You will definitely raise the price once you hit the mass market.

c) **Pre-orders collection mechanism** – If you want to create a page for collecting pre-orders quickly, we recommend you use Gummroad.com. They have a great platform with a simple interface, and sensible steps for customers to follow. They even allow you to set release dates months in advance. You could also choose to go with Trycelery.com. They, too, have a great platform where you can collect pre-orders and even organize a crowd funding campaign.

d) **Maintaining contact** – It is extremely important that you send your customers regular updates after they have pre-ordered your product. This can be in the form of weekly emails that give them progress reports and allow for inquiries to be made. You can also choose to set up a private group on Facebook for your pre-order customers to interact, discuss, and share progress and feedback. Do not take people's money and then just leave them clueless as to what is going on.

e) **Minimum number of prospects for validating the project** – How many people do you need to pre-order before you decide to start production? Not everyone you talk to will agree to pre-order your product, even if they know the solution suits them. The so-called early adopters usually form a small group, with the majority coming in somewhere in the middle, and the laggards bringing up the rear of the curve. For our case, we don't need a large majority to pay us upfront because we are still validating the idea. The best standard to use is 10% of the prospects you pitch to. If you manage to speak to 100 prospects, you should expect at least 10 people willing to pre-order your product. You may not even have to talk to as many as 100 people. Remember that this is an experiment to see whether the market is going to be interested, so don't try to get everyone on board.

f) **Failure to reach the minimum target** - You have to be prepared for the eventuality that you may not meet your minimum validation requirement. If you cannot get 10 people to buy into your idea, don't lose hope. An entrepreneur must learn to fail at things so that they can figure out how to do it right. Use this as a learning process, figure out what turned your customers off, change things, and then repeat the process. How do you find out what went wrong? Ask your prospects! You have their email addresses already, so send them an email inquiring as to why they were not interested. Do not be afraid of making this bold step because your prospects may be having some vital piece of information that can change your failure into success. If you receive some negative responses, don't take them personally. Instead of wasting time dealing with unfair criticism, just get back to work and improve your business.

By now you should be confident that you possess all the necessary skills for validating any business idea that you may have. In the next chapter, we are going to examine some examples of how you can put these four validation steps into practice.

CHAPTER 16: EXAMPLES OF VALIDATION

In the previous chapter, we learned about the steps that you have to go through when validating your idea. Let's remind ourselves of what they were:

#1: Gain access to your audience

#2: Hyper focus target

#3: Engage in active interactions

#4: Make the sale

This chapter contains some concrete examples of how entrepreneurs can manage to execute the four steps above to validate whatever business ideas they have. We have tried to get samples from a diverse range of business markets. Each example is aimed at breaking down each step of the validation process.

One thing we would like to point out is that though we have given a set structure for validating your idea, you are at liberty to use your own creativity when it comes to mode of execution. We will try to show you this in the examples below.

Let's get going!

EXAMPLE 1: JOHN'S MOTIONS GRAPHICS IDEA

Step 1: Gain access to your audience
John has been uploading motion graphics tutorial videos on his YouTube channel and has so far managed to accumulate a small group of subscribers. He discovers that there are many people looking for tutorial videos about animations and decides to sell animation software. However, he learns that this business idea isn't in line with his passion, so he focuses more on educating and training people about animations. John decides to start creating and selling a course. Rather than spending at least three months creating the course, he decides to first determine if anyone is going to be interested in his idea.

Step 2: Hyper-Target
John's tutorial videos contain a call-to-action for viewers to subscribe to his channel. As people begin to subscribe to join his email list, he begins to get a feel of the level of interest about animations, and whether people enjoy his teaching methods.

Step 3: Engage and interact with the audience
John opts to send everyone on his list an email. In the email, John is honest with the audience and tells them about his background with animation. He explains how he used to be terrible at creating animations and had no formal training in it. He talks about his fear of not being good enough, until the day he discovered the principles and rules that can help anyone become a better animation artist. He offers to teach a few members these principles in exchange for some amazing perks.

See what happened there? John manages to connect with his email subscribers on a personal level by simply telling them the truth. He doesn't BS them about being some expert with superb qualifications. This would most likely alienate many people who are struggling to create animations with little formal education. His aim is to show his audience that he can relate to them. He also makes sure to inform his audience about his plan to begin the course with just a small group of 20, with each spot going for $200.

John proceeds to setup a webinar, and after realizing a high level of interest, he chooses to start developing the training course.

Step 4: Make the sale
John begins the webinar by spending the first 30 minutes providing the audience with free tips and techniques that they will find useful. This ensures that even those who choose not to join his program gain from the webinar. On top of that, he shows his audience the kind of stuff they should expect from his course. He spends the last 20 minutes talking about the animation course, informing the audience that it wasn't developed yet and that the early adopters would help him to perfect it.

Once he shares the call-to-action, he sells out all the 20 spots within minutes and earns $4,000. A few days later, he decides to expand the group to 40 people and sends his subscribers an email. The 20 additional spots sell out within minutes. The early adopters love the course and write glowing testimonials. John even manages to sell the next training course at $600 per person and still sells out 75 spots!

EXAMPLE 2: ANNA'S VIRTUAL YOGA IDEA

Anna works as an attorney who wants to start her own business. She has an idea about doing something related to the yoga industry because she is passionate about yoga. She decides to do some market research by sending some of the small yoga business owners emails. She requests an opportunity to call them and talk about some of the biggest needs and problems they have. She receives a 95% response rate and manages to call more than 70% of the business owners. The phone calls allow her to get ideas about how to create her business.

One of the reasons for her high response rate was her assurance that each business owner would receive a summary of a report about the information she would collect from everyone. This encouraged the business owners because they would benefit from the information as well.

One of the major needs of the majority of the owners was trying to take their yoga classes online. They wanted to do it but didn't even know where to start. Once Anna had figured out her target business idea, she started the validation process.

Step 1: Gain access to your audience

In Anna's case, her audience would be the yoga business owners that she contacted via email and phone.

Step 2: Hyper-Target
Once she had her target idea in mind, Anna contacted the business owners who had expressed the desire to take their yoga classes online. She had an easy time doing this because she had already established a rapport with them. She used the conversations to refine her idea and specify exactly what the audience wanted.

Step 3: Engage and interact with the audience
Anna shared her potential idea with a few of her target audience, informing them that she was ready to create the software if there was a high level of interest. She was pleasantly surprised when one of the business owners offered to pay her upfront even before he saw the product! It was at that moment that Anna realized that people were willing to pay for the software. She went ahead and created a wireframe for her product and used it to visually demonstrate how it would work.

Step 4: Make the sale
After she had created the wireframe, she contacted the rest of the business owners and offered to demonstrate the software. Her goal was to show them what the final product would look like and see whether there was enough interest from the audience. Anna was able to build the software and use it to help the yoga studios setup their classes on the internet. The rest, as they say, is history!

Well, we've come this far, and to be honest, you have done extremely well to stick around until now. Congratulations!

There is a lot of information that we have covered so far. We started out by setting aside your idea and first considering what you really wanted from life. Most people never consider what makes them tick, and you did great by looking inward and opening up yourself.

Then we dived into creating a mind map to define your specific ideas and learning to share your ideas with strangers. Overcoming this fear is never easy, but you just have to know how to manage it.

The next step was creating a Customer P.L.A.N. and understanding your target market. This is something that you can still use as your business continues to grow. You discovered what the solutions for customer problems were, and even put one of your solutions through the validation process.

It's time to go into the final chapter. It's a short summary of some of the tips that you need to know as we close.

CHAPTER 17: PREPPING FOR YOUR LAUNCH

It takes a lot to get to where you are right now, seated on the cusp of greatness. You didn't start out with much knowledge but now you have more information about your market than you ever dreamed possible. This has given you the confidence and direction few entrepreneurs ever have when starting out.

As you prepare to launch your business, you must use the momentum you have built to propel you further ahead. You are now ready to set up a full-scale business. However, don't forget to take it step by step, always checking and adjusting your course.

Listed below are five tips that will help you on your entrepreneurial journey.

1. Break Down Your Business Process and Learn to Appreciate Small Wins

Nobody said it would be easy building a thriving business. Since most entrepreneurs are extremely ambitious, you will start to put a lot of pressure on yourself, trying to achieve your big goals. However, this can lead you into a trap where you want everything to be perfect and fail to get anything done.

If you have a goal that is so big it scares you into paralysis, the best thing to do is break it down into smaller pieces that you can work on individually. This will make your work less intimidating. Every time you finish one piece of the project, you should celebrate your progress. This will give you the motivation to keep going.

Remember to set big goals for your business, break them down into manageable sizes, and appreciate every milestone you achieve.

2. Find People Who Support You
Successful entrepreneurs are always surrounded by people who believe in their business. This may or may not involve hiring staff or building a team. However, having a support system is critical to achieving success. You need to have people in your life who believe in your dream. For some of you, this won't be easy, especially when you are just in the beginning phases of your business. Family members and loved ones may sometimes fail to offer the moral support an entrepreneur needs to stay motivated and inspired. It may be difficult to convince them your idea is worth it and may even cause strife among relatives.

Don't worry if you cannot get support from your loved ones. You should connect with other entrepreneurs and form a group where you can exchange ideas and hold each other accountable. Make sure that your group has smart and ambitious business people that are willing to help each other succeed.

3. Your Customers Are Precious
As an entrepreneur, whether you have followers, customers, viewers, subscribers, or listeners because these people are extremely precious to your business. You should be careful that you do not forget the value

of these people as your business grows. They are not just numbers that symbolize how much money you are making. Treat them well because they are precious to your business.

The beauty of the beginning phases is that you enjoy the benefits of a small business. It is easier to engage with customers and maintain human connections with them. You are better off than the larger companies that don't even have time to respond to customer emails.

Finally, don't forget to surprise your customers every once in a while. Do something unique and memorable for them. They will stay loyal to you.

4. Never Forget Why You Are An Entrepreneur
What you do and how you do it are important things to keep in mind. However, what eventually keeps you going is remembering why you are an entrepreneur in the first place. You have come a long way in this book, but why did you bother? What is the reason you are doing this? There is only one person who can answer that question – You.

As you continue with building and growing your business, your mind will have many different issues to deal with. You are going to forget the fundamental reasons for starting your own business. Remember the Future Test you did in Chapter 2? Find that piece of paper and look at the things you wrote down. This piece of paper should always be nearby so you can remind yourself of the lifestyle and person you desire to be.

5. Enjoy Your Journey
Being an entrepreneur can be hectic, stressful, and challenging. As you deal with failures and successes, ensure that you enjoy your journey. You have chosen the path least traveled.

We wish you all the success in your business! Thank you!

CONCLUSION

As we reach a close, you need to know that no matter what happens with your original business idea, you can make it as an entrepreneur. Yes, you may have validated your idea, but the truth is that you have also validated yourself.

Entrepreneurship is taking a risk, learning from your mistakes, and moving one step forward. Do not give up no matter how hard it gets. You have been very patient reading every page of this book, and all you have to do now is stay committed to building your business.

Make sure that you use the steps and processes outlined here. They will help you create a strong foundation when you are starting your business. This wasn't just theoretical advice that has never been tested in real life. If you make good use of the information in this book, you will stand a better chance of succeeding as an entrepreneur.

We wish you all the best.

Good luck!

THANKS FOR READING

We hope you enjoyed this book. If you found this material helpful, please share it with a friend you know would love it too.

You can also help others find it by leaving a review where you purchased the book. Your feedback will help us continue to write books you love. Your one simple act of sharing could change someone else's life. Just so you know, the Entrepedia library is growing by the day so be sure to check out some of the other awesome books we offer. We recommended a few for you to start with on the last page of this book.

Also, we would love to hear your thoughts personally. Email us at feedback@entrepedia.co and let us know how we can improve our books.

Tell us, what it would take for us to create something you would want to tell everyone you know about?

Thanks

Remember
Receive 5 FREE Entrepreneur books by visiting
www.Entrepedia.co/FREEbooks

Get Your Entrepreneur Quick Start Guide here
www.Entrepedia.co/QuickStart

OUR MISSION

Entrepreneur Encyclopedia aims to accelerate the availability of useful information and aims to publish a high quality insightful book on every major topic in entrepreneurship.

Entrepedia hopes to remove barriers in sharing by taking the copyright off everything we publish and donating it to the public domain. We believe Copyright is hinders the sharing of information and ideas and instead only promotes a scarcity mindset. We hope other publishers and authors will follow our example. In addition, it is our goal to donate $1,000,000 or more by 2020 to help people in emerging nations access the capital they need to build fresh water systems, create a startup economy and enhance their local communities through entrepreneurship.

Doesn't it feel good knowing that as you educate yourself you are helping the world become a better place? We think so too.

Cheers to an epic future!

Travis and the Entrepedia Team

WHY ENTREPRENEUR ENCYCLOPEDIA WAS STARTED

Every time I wanted to capture a complete grasp of something new I'd have to buy 20 books on the topic and spend way too long sorting through them and everything online until I arrived at the big picture or receive any actionable insight.

I wished someone else would go in and figure out which information would impact me most and present it to me so I could quickly and easily devour it then apply it to my business. I couldn't find anyone doing this with quality in the entrepreneur space and figured I would just have to do it myself.

I wanted Entrepreneur Encyclopedia to curate the most helpful content in the field and put the best of the best information in little packets on every subject imaginable. I also wanted the topics to be readable within half an hour. That way I would be able to make time to read one or more books a day and fill my idea jar with knowledge.

By creating and sharing these books, Entrepreneur Encyclopedia aims to save you time and money. My team and I do all the research up front so you don't have to. Our goals is to sort through the best content on each topic, extracting the most complete understanding possible in under 30 minutes.

The quicker we can learn a wide variety of topics the sooner that information can begin playing a role in shaping our results now. And all the better if we can also make a positive difference in the world while doing it. That's why I focus on entrepreneurship and giving back. I know how hard it is starting from scratch so I'm donating 5% of this company's profits to fund micro loans from people with a vision but don't qualify for traditional funding.

We're also planting a tree for every 10 hard covers we sell and challenging ideas about copyright's place in today's world. As a company we have to be doing everything we can to support the ecosystem we all live in. I hope you join me in making this possible by supporting Entrepreneur Encyclopedia.

Thanks for reading,

Travis

If you enjoyed this book, you might also like Smart Reads

Smart reads delivers the same **compact information books** on a wide variety of topics outside of entrepreneurship. Here are a couple books you might find helpful:

The 30-Day Focus Plan: Achieve Laser Focus and Cut Through Noise in this Distracting World

Twitter Marketing Strategies: Smart Tips on How to Monetize Your Followers

How to Master Email Marketing: Your 1-Page Marketing Plan to Grow a Massive Email List, Make Money and Build Your Brand with Email

Writing on the Internet: Learn SEO Tips & Techniques and Become a Successful Online Writer

Change Your Mind Change Your Life: Control Your Life By Changing The Way You Think

Overcoming Procrastination: Proven Strategies on How To Improve Focus, Get Things Done and Achieve Your Goals

www.ingramcontent.com/pod-product-compliance
Lightning Source LLC
Chambersburg PA
CBHW050112230526
45470CB00004B/1789